in tribute to saroj Fleming, MD
who takes beautiful pictures of her babies.

□ □ □ □ □ □ □ □ □

MY BROTHER & ME

THE ADVENTURES OF MAX AND LEO

written by Judi Taylor Cantor

illustrated by Mary Kate Gaide

design by Laura goldberg

■ ■ ■ ■ ■ ■ ■ ■ ■ ■ my brother Leo is

FUN.

he likes to **JUMP** on me.

i love BROCOLLI.

i teach leo how to

S L I D E

down the
banister.

Leo thinks roses smell like **PEANUT BUTTER.**

i think roses smell like

HAPPINESS.

i show Leo how to
put the
water bottle

NOZZLE

in our

NOSES.

i am an

ARTIST.

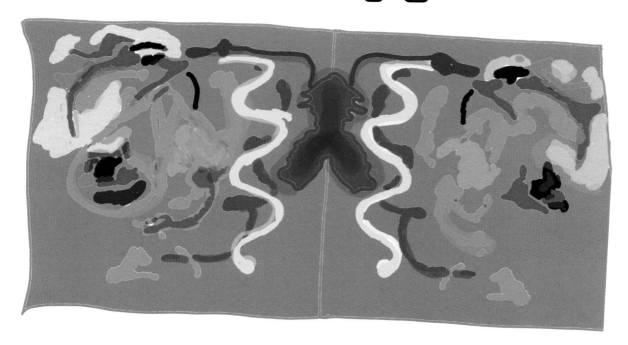

Leo thinks my paintings are

BEAUTIFUL.

cracker and salami mustaches
make me **BURP.**

I should
go to finishing

SCHOOL.

I get to show Leo
how to eat ripe

RASPBERRIES

off the

TREE.

i like to play
DRESS UP with **COSTUMES.**

20

So does Leo. Sometimes he is a

KNIGHT.

we like to play

MUD
MAN.

Leo
LAUGHS
&
LAUGHS.

i can show Leo how to

PLAY

with the new

TRAIN

T·U·N·N·E·L.

Leo and I have a lot of **FUN** with homemade **SILLY** putty.

When it's time for

BED

I read him a

STORY.

28

Leo is my BEST friend.
my BROTHER.